Pig Chinese Horoscope 2024

By

IChingHun FengShuisu

Table of Contents

Introduce

The character of people born in the year of the PIG

People born in this year are wise, trustworthy, kind-hearted, generous, and selfless. It's not a big deal if whoever sees it loves and gets along with others easily. You are cautious, attentive, and brave; try to put your trust in me. You'll know they're so good at doing everything right and never disappointing you. People born in the Year of the Pig are universally adored. People born in this year are born to serve and to give. The majority of people take advantage of this opportunity. Even as they get older, people born in the Year of the Pig don't feel bad about it. People born in the Year of the Pig continue to believe that everyone is born with a good heart. People born in this year are willing to forego their happiness to be good friends who value manners. People who do not know people born in the Year of the Pig well may believe they are unethical. And she enjoys eating chocolate after dinner, which she always overdoes. People born in this year are sensitive, sweet, innocent, affectionate, romantic, and occasionally jealous.

Strength:

People born in the Year of the Pig are gentle, forgiving, and unconcerned about minor issues.

Weaknesses:

People born in this year tend to trust people who are easy to follow and do not have their ideas.

Love:

People born in this year are charming and serious about everything, but they are not as sincere in love as they should be. You like people all over the place, and if you like someone, you'll have to flirt with them. The good-looking kind Please do not approach me. In marriage and love, a woman born in the Year of the Pig outperforms a man. That is, if you meet your true soul mate, you should leave. The young woman will not waste herself or her heart for anyone other than the young pig. Will not stop there, as a result, finding a serious person can be difficult. Ancient texts say that most women born in the Year of the Pig tend to have a younger partner.

Suitable Career:
People born in this year are charming and serious about everything, but they are not as sincere in love as they should be. You like people all over the place, and if you like someone, you'll have to flirt with them. The good-looking kind Please do not approach me. In marriage and love, a woman born in the Year of the Pig outperforms a man. That is, if you meet your true soul mate, you should leave. The young woman will not waste herself or her heart for anyone other than the young pig. Will not stop there, as a result, finding a serious person can be difficult. Ancient texts say that most women born in the Year of the Pig tend to have a younger partner.

Year of the PIG (Wood) | (1935) & (1995)

"The PIG is in Dhamma Place" is a person born in the year of the PIG at the age of 89 years (1935) and 29 years (1995)

Overview

Because the planets that orbit your destiny house this year are "Dao Ngwe Tek" (Dao Chan Wasana), this year is a comfortable year for the senior destiny lord around this age. Suitable for sleeping, soothing the mind, and looking after your physical health to stay strong, as well as paying attention to diet and nutrition. Be wary of allergies and reoccurring diseases. As a result, you should schedule a morning stroll for mild exercise and routinely make merit by giving alms to the Buddha and paying devotion to the Buddha. Then, in the end, life will be joyful and tranquil.

For Destiny, 29, this is yet another year in which she must live her life carelessly. This is due to the planets "Hua Kai star" (unstable star), "Diao Khae star" (funeral guest), and "Xiaoying star" (young person) that will all come and go to irritate the house of fate, frequently resulting in unanticipated mishaps. Work, especially commercial enterprise, can generate errors and damage due to the abilities of servants or subordinates. You may also be affected by the loss of elderly relatives. However, there is good fortune in adversity because of the auspicious star "Ngwe Tek" (the moon of fortune) that revolves around us. This is enough to help transform a heavy substance into a lighter one. Work, on the other hand, will be a heavy and exhausting weight. You must still assist yourself and cannot rely on others. This year, you must be persistent in lobbying and courageous in confronting hurdles. For results to occur, both must be devoted and work hard. If you sit motionless with your hands and feet bowed, everything will move backward. So act now and don't let time pass you by in vain.

Career and Business

The quality of this year's work is poor. There will be disagreements inside the organization. You must also be wary of abrupt changes and transfers in the workplace. Working now needs patience and perseverance. You should be careful during the following months that work will cause obstacles and problems, namely: 1st Chinese month (4 Feb. - 4 Mar.), the 4th Chinese month (5 May - 4 Jun.), the 7th Chinese month (7 Aug. - 6 Sep.) and 10 Chinese month (7 Nov. - 5 Dec.), famous periods. Work must be thoroughly examined and advice offered to subordinates to avoid harm. When signing a contract or starting a new job, you must be wary of swindlers who create luxurious projects to fool you. In addition, beginning a new career or forming a joint venture. You must be cautious not to be duped by fraudsters and create difficulties and harm. As for the months when work and business experience smooth progress, they include the 2nd Chinese month (5 Mar. - 3 Apr.), the 6th Chinese month (6 Jul. - 6 Aug.), the 8th Chinese month (7 Sept. – 7 Oct.) and the 9th Chinese month (8 Oct. – 6 Nov.).

Financial

This year's financial fortunes will be a combination of excellent and terrible. Windfalls can bring you money. However, you must be wary of unforeseen charges that can drain your bank account. What you should avoid this year is being duped into investing in shady or illegal enterprises. Because there is a possibility of a criminal prosecution this year. This year, the months that your finances will be disrupted include the 1st Chinese month (4 Feb. - 4 Mar.), the 4th Chinese month (5 May - 4 Jun.), the 7th Chinese month (7 Aug. - 6 Sep.) and the 10th Chinese month (7 Nov. - 5 Dec.) During this time, exercise caution while investing money in many sectors. Be careful not to let greed cloud your judgment of reality. To maintain liquidity, you should also control your income and spending.

As for the months where finances are flowing smoothly, they are the 2nd Chinese month (5 Mar. - 3 Apr.), the 6th Chinese month (6 Jul. - 6 Aug.), the 8th Chinese month (7 Sep. – 7 Oct.) and the 9th Chinese month (8 Oct. – 6 Nov.).

Family

This year has been both wonderful and difficult for the family. There will be increased turbulence, quarrels, and confrontations in the house. You must both be concerned about the safety of your family members. Accidents will occur both at work and when traveling. It is essential to pay close attention to the health of the elderly at home. Especially during the months when your family will experience more chaos, including the 1st Chinese month (4 Feb. - 4 Mar.), the 4th Chinese month (5 May - 4 Jun.), and the 7th Chinese month. (7 Aug. – 6 Sep.) and the 10th Chinese month (7 Nov. – 5 Dec.) During such times, one should be patient and tolerant to look over certain problems and prevent disputes. Furthermore, be wary of kids losing things in the house or having their belongings stolen.

Love

Your love horoscope for this year has changed. It is believed that you will fall in love, flirt with someone, and have hope. However, you must be wary of the force of lust from "Dao Tho

Huai," which may drive you to feel false love. It is claimed that this year, in addition to being cautious in your relationship choices, you must also utilize your heart to exchange hearts with genuine people, which is something we truly aspire for. Avoid being a third party in someone else's relationship. Otherwise, karma will come after you. The months in which love and relationship problems can easily occur include the 1st Chinese month (4 Feb. - 4 Mar.), the 4th Chinese month (5 May - 4 Jun.), and the 7th Chinese month. (7 Aug. - 6 Sep.) and the 10th Chinese month (7 Nov. - 5 Dec.) During this period, you should avoid traveling to entertainment venues.

Health

This year's fortune teller is in good health. However, the lack of care and attention cannot be overstated. This is due to the appearance of the evil stars Xiao Khae and Xiao Ying based on health. As a result, older fortune tellers must pay additional attention and care. Try to get adequate sleep and avoid meals that are greasy, salty, or spicy. Accidents should be avoided when it comes to the young destiny. When traveling or operating a car, safety must be the priority. Especially during the months when health problems are likely to occur, including the 1st Chinese month (4 Feb. - 4 Mar.), the 4th Chinese month (5 May - 4 Jun.), the 7th Chinese month (7 Aug. - 6 Sep.), and the 10th Chinese month (7 Nov. - 5 Dec.) What is known is that alcohol and narcotics must be avoided. Because it will lead you to lose consciousness, causing difficulties with property loss and damage, as well as causing problems for your family.

Year of the PIG (Fire) | (1947) & (2007)

"The PIG is on its way" is a person born in the year of the PIG at the age of 77 years (1947) and 17 years (2007)

Overview

This year, your senior destiny will be 77 years old since the planet influencing you is the Hua Kai star (unstable star). As a result, it is essential to take care of your health to be strong, both physically and mentally, and to know how to let go. Some things irritate and anger me. Then you will be happy and feel calm and should be strict and pay special attention to your health, especially during the 1st Chinese month (4 Feb. - 4 Mar.) and the 4th Chinese month (5 May - 4 Jun.) 7th Chinese month (7 Aug. – 6 Sep.) and 10th Chinese month (7 Nov. – 5 Dec.)

For the teenage fate This year, the planets "Dao Nguy Tek" and "Dao Bun Chiang" move into your destiny house, with the influence of two fortunate stars orbiting to help you, resulting in you acquiring the power of progress. Whether studying or working, success will appear positively. Those who are studying if they are planning to take an exam or compete in any topic. There is the possibility of receiving good news and celebrating accomplishments. Some of you will be campaigning to study abroad this year, and the answer will be as predicted. However, you must be cautious between this year and things concerning family and friends. Don't be swayed by persuasions and temptations to do things you shouldn't. Hiding from the law, including immoral things, will bring danger, violence, and humiliation to the family.

Career and Business

Those destined for the Year of the Pig this year, whether for a job or education, will encounter friends who will assist and advise them along the road. Change the direction of your employment and studies. As a result, if you enhance your determination and dedication to self-development. You will undoubtedly achieve gorgeous and well-accepted success. The months that are a good time and supportive for you include the 2nd Chinese month (5 Mar. - 3 Apr.), the 6th Chinese month (6 Jul. - 6 Aug.), the 8th Chinese month (7 Sep. - 7 Oct.), and the 9th Chinese month (8 Oct. - 6 Nov.), but during the year you should be careful during the months when work and business will encounter obstacles, namely 1st month. China (4 Feb. – 4 Mar.), 4th Chinese month (5 May – 4 Jun.), 7th Chinese month (7 Aug. – 6 Sep.), and 10th Chinese month (7 Nov. - 5 Dec.) Be wary of mistakes made by members of your team that generate problems, for which you must share responsibility. Seniors must carefully check the details while signing contract paperwork. There will be no responsibilities that may affect you in the future.

Financial

This year's financial fortunes and earnings may suffer. It's because you receive little for a lot of money. As a result, the optimal approach would be to balance costs and revenue. That is, spend wisely, eliminate superfluous spending and waste, and endeavor to boost revenue to avoid a shortage of liquidity. Worrying is the potential of being duped because of your trust or being influenced by those close to you to become greedy and gamble. It is the source of property loss. During the months when finances are in decline and you must be very mindful of yourself, they include the 1st Chinese month (4 Feb. - 4 Mar.), the 4th Chinese month (5 May - 4 Jun.), the 7th Chinese month (7 Aug. - 6 Sep.) and the 10th Chinese month (7 Nov. - 5 Dec.). In addition, be careful of being dragged away, being in debt, or getting into trouble by signing financial guarantees. For the months when your finances are in a more liquid state, including the 2nd Chinese month (5 Mar. - 3 Apr.), the 6th Chinese month (6 Jul. - 6 Aug.), the 8th Chinese month (7 Sep. – 7 Oct.), and the 9th Chinese month (8 Oct. – 6 Nov.).

Family

Senior fortune tellers must be cautious of their health and be wary of unforeseen mishaps, according to family requirements. This will result in the loss of assets as a result of paying for medical care. In terms of adolescent fate, avoid disagreements and confrontations with family members. It will generate discord in the family. Especially during the months when the family will experience trouble and chaos, including the 1st Chinese month (4 Feb. - 4 Mar.), the 4th Chinese month (5 May - 4 Jun.), the 7th Chinese month (7 Aug. - 6 Sep.) and the 10th Chinese month (7 Nov. - 5 Dec.) Be careful of danger from unexpected falls or accidents. Also, be careful of valuables in your home being damaged or stolen.

This year is a good criterion that conceals bad for family and friends. When you meet a buddy, you just need to say three words. Don't express yourself entirely. If you make a buddy who is dishonest and malicious, you will endanger yourself. The months stated above, in particular, should be avoided. Be wary of friends who bend your back because they demand something from you. Do not get involved in fights or disputes amongst friends. Be wary about being drawn into litigation.

Love

This year's love for teens is half nice, half awful. What you should be wary about is expecting too much from love. When there is a sense of disappointment or when things do not go as planned. As a result, individuals may act on their feelings by degrading their lives in ways that harm their future. As a result, you must be cautious to safeguard your heart since it will weaken and impact other things, bringing harm. Especially during the month that you have to be especially careful and not be too easily enamored with temptation, namely the first Chinese month (4 Feb. – 4 Mar.), 4th Chinese month (5 May – 4 Jun.), 7th Chinese month (7 Aug. – 6 Sep.), and 10th Chinese month (7 Nov. – 5 Dec.) You must be conscious and have good mental control. Do not dishonor your life by engaging in immoral activities and vices. Because these are all penalties for self-harm.

Health

This year's destiny in both life cycles is in poor health. You should be cautious about lung, intestinal, and stomach diseases. You must exercise greater caution while dealing with the elderly. Avoid dizziness and falls when traveling outside, as they might create long-term issues with your bones and nerves. You should also pay more attention to the hygiene of your diet. Don't give in to your taste buds. It all comes down to tormenting oneself.

Accidents while driving and road use should be avoided by youthful fortune tellers this year. Particularly those who are hooked to the practice of collecting companions to go driving on the road. It may result in a lawsuit in addition to inflicting injury. The months that are not supportive and destined for both age cycles must be paid special attention to, including the 1st Chinese month (4 Feb. - 4 Mar.), the 4th Chinese month (5 May - 4 Jun.), the 7th Chinese month (7 Aug. - 6 Sep.) and the 10th Chinese month (7 Nov. - 5 Dec.).

Year of the PIG (Earth) | (1959)

" The PIG traverses the mountain" is a person born in the year of the PIG at the age of 65 years (1959)

Overview

This age cycle is considered a challenging year for anyone born in the Year of the Pig. As a result, another year has passed in which various labor activities are carried out. You must be patient and composed. Every action you perform must be patient. As a result, it will be secure. This is because each house of destiny is flanked by unfortunate stars that convey negative energy. This will expand its effect, leading to the fate owners frequently encountering hurdles, disagreements, and finding ways through which to bully one another. Work cannot be done in a single sitting.

In a commercial company, there are frequent disagreements, discussions are difficult, and every method must be employed to battle and win. The financial side will fall and become stuck, possibly even reaching crisis proportions. As a result, you must carefully manage your income and spending from the start of the year. Arguments and quarrels are common inside the family. In terms of health, avoid damage to your hands or legs, as well as frequent, uncomfortable headaches. Financially, there aren't many costs for this year, so you may buy things you enjoy, or a gold necklace or a gold bracelet as a gift to yourself as a cure for periods when you're losing money. The most serious issue, however, is likely to be health issues and injuries from accidents. As a result, these two factors are regarded as the most significant, and you should exercise greater caution to be safe.

Career and Business

For the fortune teller, this age cycle is seen as a year in which you must endure with patience. Work may entail shifting roles or switching job responsibilities. Subordinates who covertly saw off chair legs should be avoided. Be wary of subordinates or subordinates that conduct embezzlement, dishonesty, or make blunders that harm you and the organization. Especially during the months that work will encounter many obstacles and problems, including the 1st Chinese month (4 Feb. - 4 Mar.), the 4th Chinese month (5 May - 4 Jun.), the 7th Chinese month (7 Aug. - 6 Sep.) and the 10th Chinese month (7 Nov. - 5 Dec.) The Lord of Destiny must be more cautious, insist on meticulous inspection to reduce mistakes and use prudence while forming contracts. You will be at a disadvantage, and you should be wary of being a victim of fraud. For the months when work and investment return to a smoother direction, they are: 2nd Chinese month (5 Mar. - 3 Apr.), the 6th Chinese month (6 Jul. - 6 Aug.), the 8th Chinese month (7 Sep. – 7 Oct.) and the 9th Chinese month (8 Oct. – 6 Nov.).

Financial

This year has been a bad one for financial fortunes due to wealth loss. To limit the power of wasting money, it is recommended to buy things you like at the start of the year. Especially during the months when there will be unexpected expenses and financial downturns, including the 1st Chinese month (4

Feb. - 4 Mar.), the 4th Chinese month (5 May - 4 June), the 7th Chinese month (7 Aug. - 6 Sep.), and the 10th Chinese month (7 Nov. - 5 Dec.) During these months, lending money or signing financial commitments is banned. You should never invest in shady or unlawful enterprises. For the months in which your finances will come back bright and prosperous: 2nd Chinese month (5 Mar. - 3 Apr.), the 6th Chinese month (6 Jul. - 6 Aug.), the 8th Chinese month (7 Aug. Sept. – 7 Oct.) and the 9th Chinese month (8 Oct. – 6 Nov.).

Family

This year's family has been both nice and awful. Worrying is an unexpected event. Whether there is an issue with home safety, risks from the electrical system, electrical appliances, gasses, or items put in the home. There is a possibility of triggering an accident. As a result, if you have time, please rush to examine and repair for the welfare and safety of the home members. During the months that problems will occur within the family, they include: the 1st Chinese month (4 Feb. - 4 Mar.), the 4th

Chinese month (5 May - 4 Jun.), the 7th Chinese month (7 Aug. - 6 Sep.), and the 10th Chinese month (7 Nov. - 5 Dec.) Furthermore, you should be wary of children or subordinates who cause issues and disturbance. Be wary about things being destroyed or stolen, and expect squabbles among family members.

Love

This year's love connections will be bittersweet since the destined person will be temperamental and irritable, easily angered, and prone to arguing. Some things are minor, but if you stress them out too much, they become major. When debating, you tend to point out and shame the other person's flaws. As a result, if one party agrees to stop first and go away. Everything will be alright if you calm down a little and then think carefully and utilize your awareness to solve difficulties. During the months when your love is quite fragile include the 1st Chinese month (4 Feb. - 4 Mar.), the 4th Chinese month (5 May - 4 Jun.), the 7th Chinese month (7 Aug. – 6 Sep.) and the 10th Chinese month (7 Nov. – 5 Dec.) Be careful of offensive or offensive words. It will cause the other party to be ashamed and be the cause of division.

Health

Be wary of lung difficulties, as well as damage to the hands or legs, in this year's destined individual. Be cautious of unforeseen mishaps while working or traveling, as well as silent diseases that may arise and endanger you without your knowledge. The months during which you should pay more attention to your health include the 1st Chinese month (4 Feb. - 4 Mar.), the 4th Chinese month (5 May - 4 June), the 7th Chinese month (7 Aug. - 6 Sep.) and the 10th Chinese month (7 Nov. - 5 Dec.). This year, however, you should keep an eye out for any irregularities in your body. If you see a lump, experience regular discomfort in any place, constantly cough, or feel disoriented. You should consult a doctor right away for a checkup and treatment.

Year of the PIG (Gold) | (1971)

" The Pig is in the Coop." is a person born in the year of the PIG at the age of 53 years (1971)

Overview

Around this era, persons born in the Year of the Pig Because the planets influencing your fate this year are "Dao Hua Khai" This year, every job action that moves forward should not be impatient; instead, ponder before doing. Because if you do anything without thinking about it, mistakes will occur, requiring you to clean up and wipe it afterward. It may harm work, cause consumers to lose faith, generate difficulties, disrupt the circulation system, and result in a financial catastrophe. But only in the sense that bad things can turn into good. If you have the opportunity this year, search for helpers or instruct your children or grandkids to assist you with the labor. It will make this year's work or business go more smoothly. The younger generation's approaches and ideas will complement and develop the business, resulting in increased revenue. There is a sizable profit. It's because your destiny needs more power this year to help in the gaps. If you can discover a suitable candidate. It will make work and other activities go more smoothly.

Career and Business

The monsoon winds have had an impact on this year's operations. Your job will present challenges and troubles. Businesses will have numerous difficult difficulties waiting for you to solve them. Be cautious throughout the line of command, where you may meet transfers and changes in positions like lightning strikes. To reduce disagreements and conflicts, fulfill your obligations to the best of your abilities and do not interfere with the work of others. Especially during the months when work and trade will encounter many obstacles and problems, including the 1st Chinese month (4 Feb. - 4 Mar.), the 4th Chinese month (5 May - 4 Jun.), the 7th Chinese month (7 Aug. – 6 Sep.) and the 10th Chinese month (7 Nov. – 5 Dec.)

Be wary of being bullied or having minors give you problems at this time. Be cautious when signing contracts since there might be hidden intentions that cause difficulties later. As a result, before signing any paper, you should double-check it. Caution is advised while participating in joint ventures this year. Because you will confront accounting and administrative corruption, as well as crooked partners. Furthermore, you should avoid investing during such unfavorable months since you will most likely be duped till you lose money. As for the months in which your work and business will change for the better, these are the 2nd Chinese month (5 Mar. - 3 Apr.), the 6th Chinese month (6 Jul. - 6 Aug.) 8 Chinese month (7 Sep. – 7 Oct.) and 9 Chinese month (8 Oct. – 6 Nov.).

Financial

This year's financial fortunes are average. Even during the year, there will be some luck and revenue from supplementary jobs. However, if there is a lack of cautious spending and solid financial planning, it may have to go in the blink of an eye, leaving nothingness. Especially during the months when unexpected expenses will be found dragging money into your pocket, including the 1st Chinese month (4 Feb. - 4 Mar.), the 4th Chinese month (5 May - 4 Jun.), the 7th Chinese month (7 Aug. - 6 Sep.) and the 10th Chinese month (7 Nov. - 5 Dec.).

Family

Family horoscopes are said to be half good and half bad. However, if you can plan any auspicious activities within the house this year, it will assist the house in having auspicious energy, lessen bad luck, and reduce some of the threats of leaking and property loss. The destined person will adopt a way to compensate for the loss of riches by purchasing items he enjoys at the start of the year, such as gold for jewelry or saving for investment. It is yet another solution to the dilemma of diminishing fortune and financial loss. The months during which you need to be more careful about safety and accidents in the home include the 1st Chinese month (4 Feb. - 4 Mar.), the 4th Chinese month (5 May - 4 Jun.), the 7th Chinese month (7 Aug. - 6 Sep.) and the 10th Chinese month (7 Nov. - 5 Dec.) Be more cautious about home safety, especially electrical cables, electrical appliances, gas stoves, and other installations that, if damaged, should be fixed as soon as possible to keep them in excellent working order. Minor staff who cause difficulty or quarrels should also be avoided.

Love

The love connection in the Year of the Pig at the start of the year is frequently quarrelsome. Be wary of altering your thoughts about your boyfriend or spouse. Because of the risk zone "Sok Mok" (loneliness and desertion), if you want to discover a simple remedy, simply set aside time to take your loved one on a one-on-one excursion to alter the outside atmosphere. Eating out, going to make merit, or taking a sightseeing vacation to the provinces or foreign nations will all help to mend and heal your relationship to some level. However, it must be genuine and based on consistency. For the months when love is quite fragile and you should be careful of problems causing conflict, including the 1st Chinese month (4 Feb. - 4 Mar.), the 4th Chinese month (5 May - 4 Jun.)

7th Chinese month (7 Aug. - 6 Sep.) and 10th Chinese month (7 Nov. - 5 Dec.) To prevent the incidence of conflicts, avoid using angry words and feelings that may be directed at the other person.

Health

Your physical health is regarded as ordinary. Because of the shifting weather circumstances, you may become unwell. If you know how to take care of yourself, eat healthily, and get adequate relaxation and sleep. Don't let work stress you out. You must be able to let go and make time for exercise. It will assist in establishing a stronger immune system than taking vitamins. However, during the following months, you should be more careful and attentive to your health: 1st Chinese month (4 Feb. - 4 Mar.), 4th Chinese month (5 May - 4 Jun.), the 7th month. China (7 Aug. - 6 Sep.) and the 10th Chinese month (7 Nov. - 5 Dec.) When dining out, be wary of tainted or filthy food. Because it may lead you to get infectious infections. Food poisoning or exposure to a contagious illness occurred.

Year of the PIG (Water) | (1983)

" The Pig Lives the Forest" is a person born in the year of the PIG at the age of 41 years (1983)

Overview

This age cycle is attributable to the planets that circle into your destiny house this year for those born in the Year of the Pig. Overall, he considers this year to be another good year. Just use this year to be industrious, dedicated, and persistent, never giving up or avoiding challenges. If you put in a lot of effort, you may be rewarded handsomely. If you are willing to take risks and explore new ways to achieve your objectives. This year, there is a chance that wishes will come true as intended because many auspicious stars, including "Dao Thiang Hok" (star of the sky bestows happiness) and "Dao Nguy Tek" (star Chanwasana), are orbiting to shine in the house of destiny, all of which will spread their influence, resulting in many things that are waiting or expected to have a positive direction. You will discover sponsors in your career, especially those who conduct business, and when you are stuck, there will be those who will support and enable you to attain your desired aims. If you are considering increasing your investment, there are many occasions when it is a wonderful chance to grow your business or start your own. This year will be easier than previous ones. Both will receive a lovely and satisfactory answer. However, during the year, a set of evil stars will arrive to disrupt the house of destiny as well. "Star of the Sun" as well as "Comparison of the Sun" These two stars' power will expand, causing jealousy and being oppressed or usurped by others, whether in the trade market, clients, or other rewards. That is, the destiny owner must exercise caution since rivals will undoubtedly arrive to participate in the trade market. No one will allow us to dominate or be the single market leader in a free market. We will come into instances like these sooner or later. You just need to be prepared and devise a backup plan ahead of time to avoid being fully beaten.

Career and Business

In terms of work, it is an auspicious seat ideal for growing jobs and expanding business for the intended individual. Increasing outside investment or expanding into new company sectors will result in dividends being paid as promised. The months that work and business will be smooth and prosperous include the 2nd Chinese month (5 Mar. - 3 Apr.), the 6th Chinese month (6 Jul. - 6 Aug.), the 8th Chinese month (7 Sep. - 7 Oct.) and the 9th Chinese month (8 Oct. - 6 Nov.). During these months, you may enter stocks or invest in a variety of topics, but you must know how to select. A solid investment and entry at the perfect moment. You should also be careful during the following months that your work will encounter obstacles and you should delay various investments, including the 1st Chinese month (4 Feb. - 4 Mar.), the 4th Chinese month (5 May - 4 Jun.), the 7th Chinese month (7 Aug. - 6 Sep.) and the 10th Chinese month (7 Nov. - 5 Dec.). Furthermore, you should be aware of any communication issues inside the organization. Also, be wary of fraudsters who may try to con you out of your money. Be wary of signing a contract and being duped by persons with evil motives.

Financial

The financial fortunes of this year are not bright. However, the money expected from gambling should not be excessive. Because it may cause the money in your pocket to diminish, resulting in a liquidity crisis. Especially during the months when your finances will be disrupted, including the 1st Chinese month (4 Feb. - 4 Mar.), the 4th Chinese month (5 May - 4 June), the 7th Chinese month (7 Aug. - 6 Sep.), and the 10th Chinese month (7 Nov. - 5 Dec.) Be wary of any unexpected costs that may arise during these months. As a result, lending money to others or accepting guarantees on anyone's behalf is banned. Do not invest in unlawful enterprises, and plan your expenditures carefully from the start of the year to provide adequate financial liquidity. However, this year there are several months in which the destined person will have luck with money flowing smoothly, including the 2nd

Chinese month (5 Mar. - 3 Apr.), the 6th Chinese month (6 Jul. - 6 Aug.), the 8th Chinese month (7 Sep. – 7 Oct.) and 9th Chinese month (8 Oct. – 6 Nov.)

Family

This year brings excellent fortune to your family, and you will gain reputation, prestige, and prosperity. However, you must avoid doing anything that sticks out too much. It is hard to avoid becoming irritated by jealous people. As a result, in some scenarios, you need to minimize your part and share it with others to be the hero. You must offer credit to people who work with you; this will help many things go more smoothly. However, you must exercise caution in terms of safety and difficulties. Family members' health is especially crucial for the elderly. Especially during the months when problems and chaos arise in the family, namely the 1st Chinese month (4 Feb. - 4 Mar.), the 4th Chinese month (5 May - 4 Jun.), the 7th Chinese month (7 Aug. - 6 Sep.) and the 10th Chinese month (7 Nov. - 5 Dec.) Take precautions to ensure your family's safety at home. Be wary of people in the house having disagreements with neighbors, and be wary of items being destroyed, lost, or stolen.

Love

A suitable criterion is love for this year's destiny. Lovers better understand and care for one another. There are conditions to be lucky this year for single individuals to encounter excellent news, auspicious situations, or cheerful anecdotes about achievement in other fields instead. However, due to the impact of terrible stars throughout the year, people get into problems. As a result, you must exercise caution when it comes to inciting confrontation and aggressive disagreements. You must work on lowering your pride. The months when love is fragile and you should be especially careful are the 1st Chinese month (4 Feb. - 4 Mar.), the 4th Chinese month (5 May - 4 June), the 7th Chinese month (7 Aug. - 6 Sep.), and the 10th Chinese month (7 Nov. - 5 Dec.) Be cautious of misconceptions, and do not take rumors lightly. You should exercise good self-control over your actions and words. To avoid squabbles, be alert and regulate your emotions.

Health

In terms of overall health, this year is deemed to be healthy, or perhaps it's because people are lucky and ill and stop inquiring about it. However, one cannot be careless or careless, especially during the following months: 1st Chinese month (4 Feb. - 4 Mar.), 4th Chinese month (5 May - 4 Jun.) 7th Chinese month (7 Aug. - 6 Sep.), and 10th Chinese month (7 Nov. - 5 Dec.). Be cautious about workplace accidents. If it is caused by impatience, you will have bleeding. Furthermore, if there is a drinking party or social gathering where you will consume excessive amounts of alcohol, you should avoid driving to decrease accidents.

Chinese Astrology Horoscope for Each Month

Month 12 in the Rabbit Year (6 Jan 23 - 3 Feb 23)

The life path begins this month for people born in the Year of the Pig, with opportunities for both good and evil. Even though corporate processes have been enhanced in many areas. However, managerial and financial issues are threatening to return the situation to disarray. What you should do this month is enhance your interpersonal relationships, communicate and negotiate at work, and avoid using emotions. The storm will pass if you only wait a bit. Allow everything to return to its former glory.

Be cautious throughout this stage of employment; trust will lead to failure. You must be cautious of fraudsters who claim to act well and speak trustworthy and will fool you into losing your money or engaging in a business cycle that is dangerous to the country's legislation.

The remuneration is reasonable for this position. There is about equal quantity of getting and paying. Furthermore, if you spend freely, you run the risk of running out of money and losing your liquidity. You should also avoid gambling. You may face criminal prosecution if you participate in illicit business or infringe on the copyrights of others.

For individuals who already have a companion and lover in terms of love. There are many quarrels and quarrels about petty issues. Please, however, do not become entangled with someone else's partner or spouse. As a result, it will not exacerbate the situation.

In terms of health, you must practice good cleanliness. Drinking and eating are both harmful to the body. Both must be cautious of seasonal infectious infections and air allergies. Other ailments will emerge if you do not take care of your health. You may develop ill to the point of hospitalization.

You must carefully study information if you are starting a new career, investing in stocks, or making other investments this month.

Support Days: 4 Jan., 8 Jan., 12 Jan., 16 Jan., 20 Jan., 24 Jan., 28 Jan.
Lucky Days: 3 Jan., 15 Jan., 27 Jan.
Misfortune Days: 6 Jan., 18 Jan., 30 Jan.
Bad Days: 9 Jan., 21 Jan.

Month 1 in the Dragon Year (4 Feb 23 - 5 Mar 23)
The horoscope of persons born in the Year of the Pig swings slightly this month. Because of a meeting with a swarm of wicked stars orbiting the mansion of destiny. Things that have worked well in the past will now have a chance to change. The situation is subject to change at any time. During this month, you should focus on your obligations. You should begin cleaning up the job as soon as possible and not let it pile up. The longer you pull it, the more stuck it becomes. You should also establish positive personal relationships with others around you. Because it will be a strategy to "Make friends and reduce enemies," the risk of bullying from others is reduced. If anything unexpected happens during this period, you must know how to relax and take it easy to escape the dark risks. Remember that you are your person at all

times. Do not expect to breathe via someone else's nose.

In terms of employment, you must be wary of minors who cause difficulties with clients or agencies with whom you frequently contact. As a result, while some issues are critical, you should speak up and take action. However, if anything goes wrong and causes damage, it should not be overlooked. Because the negative ramifications will be far-reaching. Furthermore, establishing a new job, participating in joint ventures, and making various investments this month necessitates critical event analysis. Be cautious, since corruption might harm you.

In terms of money, you should be frugal this month. You should also not anticipate making a fortune from gambling or getting wealthy via the use of illicit money. Because it may not be worthwhile.

Family horoscope: Be wary about having things destroyed or stolen. Be wary of quarreling with neighbors, and be wary of little servants who cause a lot of bother. However, in terms of love, this month is favorable; you will meet someone you like who will give you advice and assistance.

Regarding relatives and friends, you must choose to associate with individuals you do not know; you have the right to meet friends who come to bother you about money or to deceive you and hope for advantages.

Support Days: 1 Feb., 5 Feb., 9 Feb., 13 Feb., 17 Feb., 21 Feb., 25 Feb., 29 Feb.
Lucky Days: 8 Feb., 20 Feb.
Misfortune Days: 11 Feb., 23 Feb.
Bad Days: 2 Feb., 14 Feb., 26 Feb.

Month 2 in the Dragon Year (6 Mar 23 - 5 Apr 23)
This month has become a supporting month for people born in the Year of the Pig. You also gain instant strength and assistance from the auspicious constellations, including the "Boon Chiang Star" and the "Hok Chae Star," which orbit to shine and shine on your future. As a

result, the horoscope curve is inclined upward, facilitating easy labor and business. Many things for which you are hoping for hope or an answer will go in a good path. This month, you should continue to learn and improve yourself to stay up with changing conditions. Finding innovative ways to generate new works, promote new items, or conceive new marketing channels to be a trading market leader before others.

During this time, you will discover elders to help you in business and life. As a result, contacting and negotiating will be simple. As a result, it is regarded as an excellent opportunity to grab the moment and speed up the project. Open new marketing channels or extend your production base to reach new consumers. Starting a new job, investing in stocks, and making other external investments are all possibilities for this month.

Financial fortune is a moment of success when money floods in and you may reap the benefits of your efforts. There is enough money to go around from gaming. However, you must not be greedy, since excessive spending will result in a shortage of money.

The family fortune is prosperous and tranquil. The happy and joyous side of love. This is also an excellent month for singles to beg for love and reconciliation. It's also a good period for engagement and marriage.

In terms of physical health, it's reasonable. If you do not take proper care of yourself at this time, you will become unwell as a result of the weather.

Support Days: 4 Mar, 8 Mar., 12 Mar., 16 Mar., 20 Mar., 24 Mar., 28 Mar.
Lucky Days: 3 Mar, 15 Mar., 27 Mar.
Misfortune Days: 6 Mar, 18 Mar., 30 Mar.
Bad Days: 9 Mar, 21 Mar.

Month 3 in the Dragon Year (6 Apr 23 - 5 May 23)
When the Year of the Pig begins, the individual must create goals and plan work to designate a budget for operations. Manpower and financial

resources are required to run the firm as intended. Because your job and business will encounter both good and terrible things this month. Every job activity should be regarded seriously. During this period, you should try your best to take care of your job without interfering with the work of others, while keeping an eye on and analyzing the surrounding circumstances. You should also prepare to be a front-line leader when the time and opportunity are perfect.

In terms of work this month, be wary of outside provocations that may spark internal disagreements, generating issues with clients or business partners you must deal with. As a result, every task should be carried out with caution, and a backup plan should be devised. Both emphasize strengths and narrow gaps to avoid mistakes and damage to the work.

It's an excellent deal in terms of money. However, if you want to gain money from fortune, you must be cautious and know how to manage your money. Don't be greedy or you'll lose your money and become a victim of fraudsters. To avoid being duped, you should not lend money to people or sign commitments.

During this period, you must be cautious and sensitive to the elderly's health and safety inside the family. This includes being cautious about potential hazards.

When traveling or driving if you are in bad condition, be cautious of heart disease, liver illness, and accidents.

Keep your distance from relatives and friends at this time, and avoid going to parties.

There is a potential that you may be duped into losing your fortune if you start a new job, invest in stocks, or make other investments this month.

Support Days: 1 Apr., 5 Apr., 9 Apr., 13 Apr., 17 Apr., 21 Apr., 25 Apr.
Lucky Days: 8 Apr., 20 Apr.
Misfortune Days: 11 Apr., 23 Apr.

Bad Days: 2 Apr., 14 Apr., 26 Apr.

Month 4 in the Dragon Year (6 May 23 - 5 Jun 23)
This month, your destiny home born in the Year of the Pig is still plagued by evil. It's because fate has shifted and discovered a path of punishment. As a result, the horoscope's orientation deviates from the orbit. Various job tasks will not proceed as planned, creating hurdles and troubles. This month, you should postpone all investments. It is critical to assess your strength and readiness before taking a job or starting employment. You cannot cross without being cautious. Small faults should not be ignored since they might grow into major mistakes.

During this time of labor, particularly in commercial companies, you must avoid making blunders or confronting big hurdles that cause stress. Both parties should use caution when accepting or hiring positions. Consider the specifics carefully if you need to work on paperwork to sign a contract. Because you may come across fraudsters who provide a false picture to take advantage of you. Furthermore, you should avoid conducting some sort of work that may violate your copyright or violate the law, causing you harm.

This salary horoscope is experiencing a loss of money. You might fix the problem by purchasing items you want at the beginning of the month. You should also refrain from all forms of gambling and fortune-telling. You must be more cautious if you must invest more in new items.

There is a lack of harmony in the household. Because members of the House frequently disagree,

There are still fights in love, and you must be careful with your words. Don't attack each other over emotions and pride; it will simply exacerbate the fissures.

In terms of your poor health during this time, you should be wary of gastritis and inflammatory bowel disease. You should not drive a car after drinking alcohol or other intoxicants since an accident may occur.

When it comes to kin, avoid interfering in other people's internal relationships.

This month is not a good time to start a new career, buy stocks, or make other investments.

Support Days: 3 May., 7 May., 11 May., 15 May., 19 May., 23 May., 27 May., 31 May.
Lucky Days: 2 May., 14 May., 26 May.
Misfortune Days: 5 May., 17 May., 29 May.
Bad Days: 8 May., 20 May.

Month 5 in the Dragon Year (6 Jun 23 - 6 Jul 23)
This month marks the beginning of the life path of persons born in the Year of the Pig. Destiny is like a weak battery, even if your physical strength is battling hard and not retreating. However, your willpower has waned and diminished. As a result, many job operations will move slowly during this time, leading tasks to be completed later than expected. It might be because, during this month, you've

encountered several barriers and challenges that don't seem to go away, leaving you exhausted and unable to go forward. So, throughout this month, gather your thoughts and regulate your mind to be solid and powerful, utilizing your might to drive your task ahead even if it is sluggish. However, you must retain consistency and never give up or withdraw from challenges. The task will be performed satisfactorily.

Work and company are moving slowly during this period, although the entire picture appears to be lethargic. But if you set your mind to it, you can succeed. As a result, I urge that you be committed to carrying out the plans you've made to the best of your ability. Another key thing to remember this month is to avoid making oneself stand out in front of others. Because others are envious and do not want us to improve.

The financial component of this month is mild. When it comes to gambling money, you must remember not to be greedy since it will not be worth it if you hope for too much and invest too much.

The family's riches are stable, and the members of the household maintain loving, happy relationships.

Do not intervene in other people's family ties out of love. Because it may have a detrimental effect on your relationship, resulting in unneeded squabbles.

In terms of health, keep an eye out for heart disease and high blood pressure. As a result, you should make time for mild exercise and pay attention to your diet to improve your immune system.

Cooperation and help were also extended to relatives and friends.

You cannot be impatient when starting a new career, investing in stocks, or making other types of investments. Before proceeding, you must thoroughly study and evaluate your readiness.

Support Days: 4 Jun., 8 Jun., 12 Jun., 16 Jun., 20 Jun., 24 Jun., 28 Jun.
Lucky Days: 7 Jun., 19 Jun.
Misfortune Days: 10 Jun., 22 Jun.
Bad Days: 1 Jun., 13 Jun., 25 Jun.

Month 6 in the Dragon Year (7 Jul 23 - 7 Aug 23)

This month's life journey has gone better than last month's. Because the zodiac house shifts to align with the alliance line. An auspicious star appears right away. This permits the past's accumulated impediments and issues to begin to resolve positively. Many work operations begin to go in the desired direction. This month, you should do the following: Preparation in a variety of areas, including finance, labor, and technology, as well as growing yourself and your job to keep up with the circumstances without pausing. If the appropriate occasion presents itself, you will be able to strive tirelessly to achieve your predetermined objective.

In terms of your financial fortune, this month will be prosperous. Whatever you put in will begin to provide results and increase in value, making it worthwhile to invest.

Because work is the way to wealth, work will progress and commerce will thrive. May you diligently modify your interpersonal skills to be kind and persistent. This month, you will earn a lot of money and be able to go on with your life.

The horoscope for the family is serene, and favorable power has arrived. Members of the house adore one other in unison and may spread smiles and warmth.

The romantic aspect is neutral. You'll be OK.

Regular exercise will help you establish a stronger immune system and maintain a healthy physique.

If you are stranded, you will still receive support and assistance from relatives and friends.

Starting a new career, investing in stocks, and making other investments this month can all go in the right way.

Support Days: 2 Jul., 6 Jul., 10 Jul., 14 Jul., 18 Jul., 22 Jul., 26 Jul., 30 Jul.
Lucky Days: 1 Jul., 13 Jul., 25 Jul.
Misfortune Days: 4 Jul., 16 Jul., 28 Jul.
Bad Days: 7 Jul., 19 Jul., 31 Jul.

Month 7 in the Dragon Year (8 Aug 23 - 7 Sep 23)
This month, your destiny requirements are still decreasing and deteriorating. Because the road of life runs into another bump, causing the graph of fate to lose its center and drift out of orbit. This month, the most essential thing you should focus on is the health and safety of your household members. Bloodshed may occur as a result of unanticipated situations. Including property loss as a result of misplaced things or theft. As a result, this month you should

prioritize home security. You must pay careful attention to the ailments of persons in the house, especially the elderly.

The general image of work and business is not as tranquil as it should be at this time. The problem you need to fix is still the most contentious subject within the agency. Be wary of confrontations that are started by a small group of individuals but have a large influence. If you find challenges in your job, you need to be silent and listen more to each other during this period of labor. Do not jump to conclusions or make modifications without first considering and listening to all viewpoints. Because this might make the job more difficult. You should also be careful of anyone who tries to take advantage of you. Because the troubles that follow will drive you to dive even lower.

This salary horoscope is not favorable. Income comes in slowly, while expenses form lengthy lines. Close relatives should not lend money or make assurances to anyone. During this period, avoid making rash judgments. It will induce capital to flow out until there is a liquidity crisis.

When it comes to bad relatives and friends, you should be cautious while making new friends. Because it might lead you in the wrong way.

Arguments are common in romantic relationships. You should also be wary of the hazards of other people's attractions and deceptions, which can make love difficult.

Be cautious of neurological disorders, stress, and bone injuries if you are in poor health.

Starting a new career, buying stocks, and making other investments are all options. This month is best avoided.

Support Days: 3 Aug., 7 Aug., 11 Aug., 15 Aug., 19 Aug., 23 Aug., 27 Aug., 31 Aug.
Lucky Days: 6 Aug., 18 Aug., 30 Aug.
Misfortune Days: 9 Aug., 21 Aug.
Bad Days: 12 Aug., 24 Aug.

Month 8 in the Dragon Year (8 Sep 23 - 7 Oct 23)
The horoscope of persons born in the Year of the Pig is improving this month. Even though the effects of the recent rainfall remain. But you can deal with it and smooth it out. Furthermore, this month you will encounter clients that come to help solve and solve difficulties till they are gone. As a result, what you should do this month is generate employment and extend your business by discovering strategies to enhance sales and money. Change the system to eliminate work delays and accelerate progress toward the desired target direction.

Your job, including your business, is possible because you have found a sponsor to assist you. As a consequence, the accumulated backlog of work can be cleared. This month is regarded as a once-in-a-lifetime brilliant professional chance. As a result, you should not let it pass without taking action. In addition to the internal structural requirements that must be controlled, you should focus on creating and strengthening connections inside the business to encourage individuals to think positively and work together to move the firm ahead. In terms of fortune, this wage is ample and sufficient to sustain labor. However, you should increase your efforts to generate more money to compensate for the missing months.

You should also carefully organize your spending and always set aside some money for savings.

Because of an auspicious star, the family's fortunes are serene. Everyone in the house was cheerful and smiling.

Relationships appear to be more tolerant and accommodating in terms of love. This month is another lucky month for proposals, engagements, and marriages.

In terms of health, avoid getting too close to the fire element. As a result, avoid fried, grilled, and fatty meals, as well as anything hot when eaten, at this time. Be cautious of infectious infections or food poisoning.

For starting a new career, buying stocks, and making different investments. This period is doable since you will meet a patron this month who will counsel and assist you.

Support Days: 4 Sep, 8 Sep., 12 Sep, 16 Sep, 20 Sep., 24 Sep., 28 Sep.
Lucky Days: 11 Sep, 23 Sep.
Misfortune Days: 2 Sep., 14 Sep., 26 Sep.
Bad Days: 5 Sep., 17 Sep., 29 Sep.

Month 9 in the Dragon Year (8 Oct 23 - 6 Nov 23)
The journey to adulthood for individuals born in the Year of the Pig has smoothed out this month. There were also three fortunate stars circling in to shine, so auspicious energy flooded the dwelling, intended for labor and growth. The trading company will have greater sales and earnings. One thing you should do this month is to take advantage of this encouraging period to work on new technologies that will help the public. Including hurrying to generate work, make sales, and develop the business for it to grow.

In terms of employment, this is another month in which you receive three powers of encouragement and assistance. Allows us to notice favorable paths or chances in front of us. If you do not act quickly and seize this excellent chance. Be wary of someone outshining you and taking your business or market share. Those of you who work full-time, if you have been sufficiently devoted in the past. This month, your job will capture your attention, and you may get promoted or have your income boosted.

Finance is also a rich ground for fortune. Income is proportional to one's work and devotion. What you have worked hard for in the past will bear fruit in this moment.

The family side is tranquil and smooth, and you will receive pleasant news from the people in the home this month, or some of you may have requirements for planning auspicious events within the house.

The romantic relationship is still going strong. You may improve your relationship by taking your lover on vacation.

In terms of good health, when people's circumstances are excellent, so will their physical and mental health.

Good fortune will bring you people who will assist you and provide you with sound counsel.

For starting a new career, investing in stocks, and making other types of investments. You have the opportunity to invest money this month. Many products will yield good results.

Support Days: 2 Oct., 6 Oct., 10 Oct., 14 Oct., 18 Oct., 22 Oct., 26 Oct., 30 Oct.
Lucky Days: 5 Oct., 17 Oct., 29 Oct.
Misfortune Days: 8 Oct., 20 Oct.
Bad Days: 11 Oct., 23 Oct.

Month 10 in the Dragon Year (7 Nov 23 - 6 Dec 23)

Your fortunes have changed around this month. The zodiac house was clouded over. Because of the movement of malice and being affected by the evil constellation that tries to torment both "Dao Kua Hu" and "Dao Pae Hu," work is being scrutinized. Businesses should use caution while having their histories investigated by legal agencies. If you have previously dodged, violated your rights, or broken the country's criminal laws. This month's rent must be paid. All work operations should be carried out truthfully, honestly, and in compliance with the law during this month. Do not defy governmental authority for fear of repercussions or a lawsuit.

You will be in a state of flux at work at this time. The greatest method is for you to do your job well. Both should maintain positive ties with colleagues at all levels. So that we may rely on and assist one another in times of need.

The horoscope for money is normal. However, there will be unanticipated interference, resulting in property damage. As a result, you should avoid investing in things that are dangerous or that you are not yet good at. Do not lend money or sign financial commitments to others. You should stay away from gambling.

There was a lot of turbulence and a lack of serenity among the family at this time. Be wary of accidents and intruders breaking into your house.

In terms of love, the general picture remains positive. However, if you leave the bright lights, you will start a fight and bring problems into the house.

In the case of bad health, be wary of old diseases that attack and new quiet ailments that appear to become a nuisance. Either the headache persists or the body hurts. Accidents must also be avoided when traveling and working.

During this time, relatives and friends will come into contact with persons who will take advantage of them.

For starting a new job, investing in stocks, and various investments this month, be careful of being tricked into losing your money.

Support Days: 3 Nov., 7 Nov., 11 Nov., 15 Nov., 19 Nov., 23 Nov., 27 Nov.
Lucky Days: 10 Nov., 22 Nov.
Misfortune Days: 1 Nov., 13 Nov., 25 Nov.
Bad Days: 4 Nov., 16 Nov., 28 Nov.

Month 11 in the Dragon Year (7 Dec 23 - 5 Jan 24)
The Year of the Pig's life path this month is favorable. However, some accumulating difficulties have not been resolved. So, this month, give yourself the power and bravery to believe optimistically and work carefully to solve challenges. What's wrong is that teachers and experience wait for the appropriate time and chance to move ahead again.

This month, there are still problems in the organization about labor, particularly commercial operations. The pressure might be rather considerable in some circumstances. As a result, the work has not yet materialized in its final form during this time. Because there is a lack of collaboration across the agencies, we must rely on the principles of our hearts and our willingness to help address the situation. It is often necessary to be the first to raise a problem to reduce confrontation.

This salary horoscope is sufficient. Although various improvements have been made. However, it was not a smooth month because income was still unknown. Furthermore, you cannot expect to make money by gambling or speculating because there is a higher risk of losing. Also, don't be greedy and hope for other people's money to avoid losing your own.

In terms of a peaceful family, the driving force that will inspire you and the strength to overcome challenges will be unity and warmth in the house.

Because the lover chooses to listen to harsh remarks from others, love horoscopes must be cautious with words. As a result, credibility must be developed to emerge. By putting an end to unreasonable and chaotic conduct

In terms of health, the body is in good shape throughout this time.

Starting a new employment, investing in stocks, and making different investments are all options. This month is doable. Choose the appropriate investment at the right moment, and you will receive dividends.

Support Days: 1 Dec., 5 Dec., 9 Dec., 13 Dec., 17 Dec., 21 Dec., 25 Dec., 29 Dec.
Lucky Days: 4 Dec., 16 Dec., 28 Dec.
Misfortune Days: 7 Dec., 19 Dec., 31 Dec.
Bad Days: 10 Dec., 22 Dec.

Amulet for The Year of the Pig
"Guan Yin is on the Dragon"

This year, those born in the Year of the Pig should set up and worship sacred things.
"Guan Yin is on the Dragon" can improve your fortune
Place it on your work or pay desk to request blessings from the Mother of Goddess for knowledge, doing things correctly, riches, and peace and tranquillity for you and your family.

A chapter in the Department of Advanced Feng Shui discusses the gods who will visit the Mia Keng (house of fate) during their annual visit. Which is a deity who may bring both good and evil things to the year's destined human. When this is the case, worshiping to increase your luck with the gods who visit your birth year is said to be good and have the most influence on you. To relied on god's power to protect him when his fortunes declined and his miseries were lessened. At the same time, you will receive blessings for your business to run smoothly and your aspirations to come true, giving you and your family success and prosperity.

Those born in the Year of the Pig or Mia Keng (horoscope) fall under the sign of the pig. In comparison to last year, your horoscope has improved this year. It's a year when your job is rather secure. Finance and investment can still grow. Those who work frequently, on the other hand, should avoid gambling and speculating. This year, you must know how to properly safeguard the chance. You should not procrastinate or make rash decisions. There will be those willing to assist in terms of decent interpersonal connections. Everything is quiet until during the middle of the year, when you may lose money due to visitors in the house. In the future, sweet love will be a terrific beginning point. In terms of health, we must be careful not to overwork and to avoid digestive system irritation. If you want to solve an issue, you should surround yourself with sacred things and wear auspicious pendants. "Guan Yin is on the Dragon" to invoke the Divine Mother's strength and prestige to bring good fortune, money, happiness, and greater prosperity. Whatever activity you choose, someone will be there to assist and support you in making it a success.

"Bodhisattva Guan Yin" or "Bodhisattva Avalokitesvara" is the most well-known and revered Mahayana Buddhist Bodhisattva. It is a Bodhisattva who is adored by Thais and Chinese people all over the world and whose influence is widespread. "Bodhisattva Guan Yin" or Guan Yin is a Buddha who is full of love and compassion for all beings where Chinese people dwell. She is a Buddha who is overjoyed and a sign of immense compassion. Buddhists revere and appreciate Her Majesty's immense benevolence in relieving suffering from all beings across the Tribhumi.
An idol of her standing atop a dragon. It is claimed that if you put it up for worship, it would have the capacity to fend off bad luck and avoid many evils. Don't let it bother you. Let this year bring you and your family nothing but pleasure, contentment, and tranquillity.

"Guan Yin is on the Dragon, worn around the neck or carried with you when traveling outside the home, both near and far." To complete your destiny with money and fortunate locations Business and trade are flourishing and developing. All year, the family is tranquil and joyful. It creates efficiency and effectiveness that is better and faster than before.

Good Direction: Northwest, Southwest, and East
Bad Direction: Southeast
Lucky Colors: Black, Blue, and Gray.
Lucky Times: 03.00 – 06.59, 13.00 – 14.59, 19.00 – 20.59.
Bad Times: 09.00 – 10.59, 15.00 – 16.59.

www.ingramcontent.com/pod-product-compliance
Lightning Source LLC
Chambersburg PA
CBHW022000170726
47994CB00021B/1353